D0423173

To *Kelli*

From MATTY

simple truths for

T E A C H E R S

new seasons™

a division of Publications International, Ltd.

Original inspirations by:
Georgann Freeman, Marie Jones, June Stevenson

Photo credits:
FPG International: Walter Bibikow; Jim Cummins; Robert Cundy; Dennis Galante; Steve Joester;
Kevin Laubacher; David McGlynn; Christian Michaels; Michael Nelson; Telegraph Colour Library;
VCG; **SuperStock; Stone:** Simon Battensby; Martine Mouchy

Louis Weber, CEO
Publications International, Ltd.
7373 North Cicero Avenue
Lincolnwood, Illinois 60712

Manufactured in China.

8 7 6 5 4 3 2 1

ISBN: 0-7853-4898-0

new seasons
a division of Publications International, Ltd.

APPROACH the school year like a prospector.
You never know what gems you will discover.

※   ※   ※   ※

GOOD TEACHERS move mountains for their students.
Great teachers show their students
how to move mountains for themselves.

simple truths: teacher

simple truths: teacher

FOLLOW WHERE the mind of a student wanders.
You might find a lesson waiting there.

✻   ✻   ✻   ✻

A WISE TEACHER shows students not *what* to do but *how* to do things. One who is taught how to learn develops a skill that is useful throughout life.

❊   ❊   ❊   ❊

LEADING a classroom is like conducting an orchestra. Learn how to fine-tune the instruments.

JUST AS an artist uses a palette to portray a scene, a teacher uses knowledge to portray the world.

Y<small>OU CANNOT</small> put a price on proficient teaching.

It is invaluable.

T<small>HE ABILITY TO SAY</small> "I don't know"
separates a good teacher from a mediocre one.
To say "Let's find out" is the mark of a great teacher.

❋　　❋　　❋　　❋

A CLASSROOM, like a garden,
needs constant care and nurturing
to produce beautiful and steady growth.

❋   ❋   ❋   ❋

simple truths: teacher

THE MOST PRODUCTIVE classrooms don't always consist of four walls and a roof. An appropriate climate for learning may be sitting on green grass under a blue sky. It may be a garden swing and a good book. It may be nothing more than a mind deep in thought.

THE OPEN MIND of a student,
like an open door, is an
invitation to enter. Proceed
with caution and respect.

✼   ✼   ✼   ✼

GREAT TEACHERS are immortalized by
the successes of their students.

❈   ❈   ❈   ❈

A GOOD TEACHER is like a patient, caring shepherd watching over an energetic, sometimes unruly flock.

simple truths: teacher

STUDENTS WHO are taught how to listen, observe, and question will possess the golden keys that unlock the mysteries of life.

TEACH YOUNG PEOPLE to believe that the impossible is possible, and you help shape future generations.

PARENTS lay the foundation for their children's lives;
teachers help support the structure.

❈   ❈   ❈   ❈

FARAWAY LANDS become closer when a teacher
bridges the distance with knowledge.

GREAT TEACHERS know the ABCs of
unlocking a student's hidden potential:
Attention, Belief, and Caring.

✻   ✻   ✻   ✻

WHEN IT COMES to multitasking, teachers outperform even the most sophisticated computers. They have better memory capacity, higher function output, and the one kind of software no computer can offer—heart.

TEACHING IS LIKE sculpting. In September, the raw material awaits, fresh and malleable. By the end of the school year, with polishing and skill, a few rare pieces will appear.

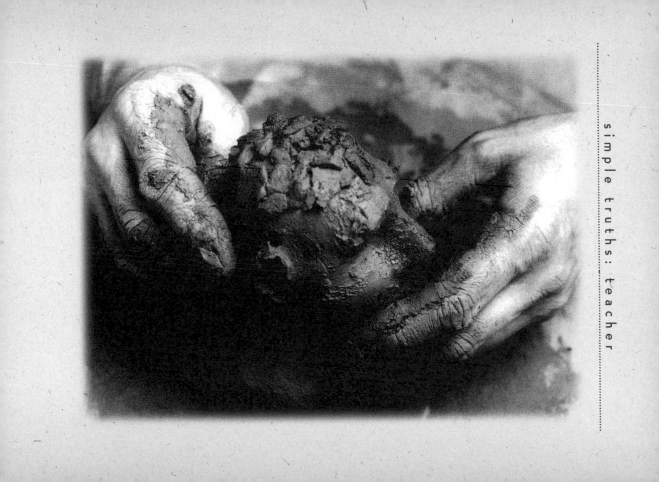

simple truths: teacher

LEARNING TO COUNT is good.

Learning what counts in life is greater.

�֍ ✖ ✖ ✖

TEACHERS POSSESS two great powers:
the ability to open and expand young minds
and control of the bathroom pass.

❈ ❈ ❈ ❈

Far beyond classrooms and school yards,
a teacher's influence lives on in the hearts of students.

WISDOM cannot be taught.
It must be cultivated.

❋ ❋ ❋ ❋

IN A CLASSROOM of restless students,
good is the teacher who can maintain order.
Great is the teacher who can capture their attention.

❈   ❈   ❈   ❈

TEACHERS TODAY are more than just instructors of various subjects. They are sages and advisors, counselors and friends, protectors and confidantes, supporters and co-creators in the visions and goals of their students.

❋　　❋　　❋　　❋

Negatives have only one place in the classroom—in the dictionary.

❋ ❋ ❋ ❋

simple truths: teacher

GOOD TEACHERS are like electricians:
They know how to light up a mind and fire up a spirit.

❈   ❈   ❈   ❈

THEY MAY NOT be paid in the millions or get huge product endorsements, but teachers get a reward no other profession offers: the opportunity to participate in the shaping of a life.

SUPPLYING information is a teacher's job.
Inspiring students to learn is a teacher's passion.

STATEMENTS OF the past and questions
of the future are entrusted to teachers,
who enlighten their students today.

✳   ✳   ✳   ✳

TEACHERS MAKE the best rulers. They are loyal to their subjects and make full use of their faculties.

Love of teaching is second only to love of learning.

A GREAT TEACHER can transform a room of bored, disenchanted students into active participants in the adventure of learning.

❋   ❋   ❋   ❋

A CLASSROOM is restricted by four walls until
a great teacher helps students break down
boundaries and grow beyond their limitations.

✳ ✳ ✳ ✳